Amazing Air Fryer Recipes

Have Fun in Your Kitchen with these Easy, Tasty and Healthy Recipes for Your Air Fryer

Linda Wang

© **Copyright 2021 by Linda Wang - All rights reserved.**

The content contained within this book may not be reproduced, duplicated or transmitted without direct written permission from the author or the publisher.
Under no circumstances will any blame or legal responsibility be held against the publisher, or author, for any damages, reparation, or monetary loss due to the information contained within this book. Either directly or indirectly.

Legal Notice:
This book is copyright protected. This book is only for personal use. You cannot amend, distribute, sell, use, quote or paraphrase any part, or the content within this book, without the consent of the author or publisher.

Disclaimer Notice:
Please note the information contained within this document is for educational and entertainment purposes only. All effort has been executed to present accurate, up to date, and reliable, complete information. No warranties of any kind are declared or implied. Readers acknowledge that the author is not engaging in the rendering of legal, financial, medical or professional advice. The content within this book has been derived from various sources. Please consult a licensed professional before attempting any techniques outlined in this book.
By reading this document, the reader agrees that under no circumstances is the author responsible for any losses, direct or indirect, which are incurred as a result of the use of information contained within this document, including, but not limited to, — errors, omissions, or inaccuracies.

TABLE OF CONTENTS

INTRODUCTION 1

Olives and Kale 5

Air Fryer Sausage 7

Sausages and Peppers 9

Blackberries and Cornflakes 11

Peppers and Lettuce Salad 13

Eggplant Bake 14

Cheesy Prosciutto and Potato Salad 16

Chicken Quesadillas 18

Cheesy Chicken Sausage Casserole 20

Amazing Hot Dogs 22

Roasted Heirloom Tomato with Feta 23

Cilantro Brussels Sprouts 25

Parmesan Zucchini Rounds 27

Amazing Onion Rings 29

Tasty Turkey Wrapped Prawns 31

Scallops with Spinach 32

Crispy Halibut 34

Simple Lime Salmon 36

Turkey and Spring Onions 38

Soy Sauce Chicken 39

Delicious Chicken Casserole 40

Chicken Tenderloins 42

Sweet and Spicy Chicken Wings 44

Chicken Kebabs 46

Honey Mustard Cheesy Meatballs 48

Lamb and Mustard Sauce 50

Pork and Chives 52

Cumin Beef 53

Pork Chops with Peanut Sauce 55

Pork Shoulder with Pineapple Sauce 58

Milanese Veal Legs 62

Broccoli with Cauliflower 65

Lentil Soup 67

Mediterranean Bamyeh Okra Tomato Stew 69

Herbed Eggplant (Vegan) 71

Grilled Buffalo Cauliflower (Vegan) 73

Greatest Green Beans (Vegan) 75

Summer Grilled Corn (Vegan) 77

Bacon Wrapped Brie 79

Garlic Cheese Dip 81

Heirloom Tomato Sandwiches with Pesto 82

Tofu in Sweet and Spicy Sauce 84

Cream and Coconut Cups 86

Apple and Cinnamon Sauce 87
Oriental Coconut Cake 88
Pound Cake with Fresh Apples 90
Crispy Good Peaches 92
Pecan Pie 94
Blueberry Muffins 97
Vanilla Pound Cake. 99

NOTES 101

INTRODUCTION

An Air Fryer is a magic revolutionized kitchen appliance that helps you fry with less or even no oil at all. This kind of product applies Rapid Air technology, which offers a new way to fry with less oil. This new invention cooks food through the circulation of superheated air and generates 80% low-fat food. Although the food is fried with less oil, you don't need to worry as the food processed by the Air Fryer still has the same taste like the food fried using the deep-frying method.

This technology uses a superheated element, which radiates heat close to the food and an exhaust fan in its lid to circulate airflow. An Air Fryer ensures that the food processed is cooked completely. The exhaust fan located at the top of the cooking chamber helps the food get the same heating temperature in every part quickly, resulting in a cooked food of better and healthier quality. Besides, cooking with an Air Fryer is also suitable for those individuals which are too busy or do not have enough time. For example, an Air Fryer only needs half a spoonful of oil and takes 10 minutes to serve a medium bowl of crispy French fries.

In addition to serving healthier food, an Air Fryer also provides some other benefits to you. Since an Air Fryer helps you fry using less oil or without oil for some kind of food, it automatically reduces the fat and cholesterol content in food. Indeed, no one will refuse to enjoy fried food without worrying about the greasy and fat content. Having fried food with no guilt is one of the pleasures of life. Besides having low fat and cholesterol, you save some amount of money by consuming oil sparingly, which can be used for other needs. An Air Fryer also can reheat your food. Sometimes, when you have fried leftover and you reheat it, it will usually serve reheated greasy food with some addition of unhealthy reuse oil. Undoubtedly, the saturated fat in the fried food gets worse because of this process. An Air Fryer helps you reheat your food without being afraid of extra oils that the food may absorb. Fried bananas, fish and chips, nuggets, or even fried chicken can be reheated to become as warm and crispy as they were before by using an Air Fryer.

Some people may think that spending some amount of money to buy a fryer is wasteful. I dare to say that they are wrong because an Air Fryer is not only used to fry. It is a sophisticated multi-function appliance since it also helps you to roast chicken, make steak, grill fish, and even bake a cake. With a built-in air filter, an Air Fryer filters the air and saves your kitchen from smoke and grease.

An air Fryer is really a new innovative method of cooking. Grab it fast and welcome to a clean and healthy kitchen.

Olives and Kale

Preparation Time: 25 minutes

Servings: 4

Ingredients:

- 4 eggs; whisked
- 1 cup kale; chopped.
- 2 tbsp. cheddar; grated
- ½ cup black olives, pitted and sliced
- Cooking spray
- A pinch of salt and black pepper

Directions:

1. Take a bowl and mix the eggs with the rest of the ingredients except the cooking spray and whisk well.
2. Now, take a pan that fits in your air fryer and grease it with the cooking spray, pour the olives mixture inside, spread

3. Put the pan into the machine and cook at 360°F for 20 minutes. Serve for breakfast hot.

Nutrition:

Calories: 220; Fat: 13g; Fiber: 4g; Carbs: 6g; Protein: 12g

Air Fryer Sausage

Preparation Time: 5 minutes

Cooking Time: 20 minutes

Servings: 5

Ingredients:

- 5 raw and uncooked sausage links
- 1 tablespoon olive oil

Directions:

1. Preheat the Air fryer to 360 degrees F and grease an Air fryer basket with olive oil.
2. Cook for about 15 minutes and flip the sausages.
3. Cook for 5 more minutes and serve warm.

Nutrition:

Calories: 131, Fat: 11.8g, Carbohydrates: 0g, Sugar: 0g, Protein: 6g, Sodium: 160mg

Sausages and Peppers

Preparation time: 0-10 minutes,

Cooking time: 15-30 minutes;

Serve: 4

Ingredients:

- 4 sausages
- 2 peppers

Direction:

1. Pour the sausages and peppers cut into pieces in the basket.
2. Cook for 20 minutes at 150 °C.

Nutrition:

Calories 339, Fat 27g, Carbohydrates 5.8g, Sugars 3g, Protein 17g, Cholesterol 84mg

Blackberries and Cornflakes

Preparation Time: 15 minutes

Servings: 4

Ingredients:

- 1/4 cup blackberries
- 3 cups milk
- 2 eggs; whisked
- 1/4 tsp. nutmeg; ground
- 1 tbsp. sugar
- 4 tbsp. cream cheese; whipped
- 1½ cups corn flakes

Directions:

1. In a bowl, mix all ingredients and stir well.
2. Heat up your air fryer at 350 °F, add the corn flakes mixture, spread and cook for 10 minutes. Divide between plates, serve and enjoy

Peppers and Lettuce Salad

Preparation Time: 15 minutes

Servings: 4

Ingredients:

- 4 red bell peppers
- 2 oz. rocket leaves
- 1 lettuce head; torn
- 1 tbsp. lime juice
- 2 tbsp. olive oil
- 3 tbsp. heavy cream
- Salt and black pepper to taste

Directions:

1. Place the bell peppers in your air fryer's basket and cook at 400 °F for 10 minutes
2. Remove the peppers, peel, cut them into strips and put them in a bowl. Add all remaining ingredients, toss and serve

Eggplant Bake

Preparation Time: 25 minutes

Servings: 4

Ingredients:

- ½ lb. cherry tomatoes; cubed
- 4 garlic cloves; minced
- 2 eggplants; cubed
- ½ cup cilantro; chopped.

- 1 hot chili pepper; chopped.
- 2 tsp. olive oil
- 4 spring onions; chopped.
- Salt and black pepper to taste.

Directions:

1. Grease a baking pan that fits the air fryer with the oil and mix all the ingredients in the pan.
2. Put the pan in the preheated air fryer and cook at 380°F for 20 minutes, divide into bowls and serve

Nutrition:

Calories: 232; Fat: 12g; Fiber: 3g; Carbs: 5g; Protein: 10g

Cheesy Prosciutto and Potato Salad

Preparation Time: 15 minutes

Servings: 3

Ingredients:

- 15 slices prosciutto; diced
- 4 pounds potatoes; boiled and cubed
- 15 ounces. sour cream

- 2 tablespoon mayonnaise
- 2 cups shredded cheddar cheese
- 1 teaspoon salt
- 1 teaspoon black pepper
- 1 teaspoon dried basil

Directions:

1. Preheat the Air Fryer to 350 - degrees Fahrenheit.
2. Combine potatoes, prosciutto, and cheddar in a baking dish. Place in the Air Fryer and cook for 7 minutes.
3. In another bowl; whisk together the sour cream, mayonnaise, salt, pepper, and basil.
4. Stir the dressing into the salad; making sure to coat the ingredients well.

Chicken Quesadillas

Preparation Time: 20 minutes

Servings: 3

Ingredients:

- 1-pound chicken breasts; boneless
- 2 soft taco shells
- 1 medium-sized onion; sliced
- 1 large green pepper; sliced
- 1/2 cup Cheddar cheese; shredded
- 1/2 cup salsa sauce
- 2 tablespoon olive oil
- Salt and pepper; to taste

Directions:

1. Preheat the Air Fryer to 370 - degrees Fahrenheit and sprinkle the basket with 1 tablespoon of olive oil.
2. Place 1 taco shell on the bottom of the fryer. Spread salsa sauce on the taco. Cut chicken breast into stripes and lay on taco shell.

3. Place onions and peppers on the top of the chicken.
4. Sprinkle with salt and pepper. Then; add shredded cheese and cover with second taco shell.
5. Sprinkle with 1 tablespoon of olive oil and put the rack over taco to hold it in place.
6. Cook for 4 – 6 minutes; until cooked and lightly brown. Cut and serve either hot or cold.

Cheesy Chicken Sausage Casserole

Preparation Time: 30 minutes

Servings: 5

Ingredients:

- ten eggs
- 2 cloves minced garlic
- 1 cup chopped broccoli

- 1 cup divided shredded cheddar
- 1/2 tablespoon salt
- 1/4 tablespoon pepper
- 3/4 cup whipping cream
- 1 [12-oz] package of cooked chicken sausage

Directions:

1. Preheat the Air Fryer to 400 - degrees Fahrenheit. Whisk the eggs in a large bowl. Add the whipping cream, and cheese and mix well.
2. In another bowl add in the garlic, broccoli, salt, pepper and cooked sausage.
3. Arrange the chicken sausage mix onto a casserole dish. Add the cheese mixture on top. Add to the Air Fryer and bake for nearly 20 minutes.

Amazing Hot Dogs

Preparation Time: 20 minutes

Servings: 4

Ingredients:

- 9 bacon fillets; raw
- 3 brazilian sausages; cut into 3 equal pieces
- black pepper to taste
- salt to taste

Directions:

1. Preheat the Air Fryer for 5 min on 355 - degrees Fahrenheit.
2. Wrap the bacon fillets around each piece of sausages then season them with some salt and pepper. Fry the wrapped sausages for 15 min then serve them and enjoy.
3. Tip: To make it tastier, sprinkle 1/2 teaspoon of Italian seasoning on the sausage pieces.

Roasted Heirloom Tomato with Feta

Preparation Time: 55 minutes

Servings: 2

Ingredients:

For the Tomato:

- 2 heirloom tomatoes
- 1/2 cup red onions; sliced paper thin
- 1 8-oz block of feta cheese
- 1 tablespoon olive oil
- 1 pinch salt

For the Basil Pesto:

- 1/2 cup parsley; roughly chopped
- 1/2 cup parmesan cheese; grated
- 1/2 cup basil; rough chopped
- 3 tablespoon pine nuts; toasted
- 1 garlic clove
- 1/2 cup olive oil
- 1 pinch salt

Directions:

1. Make the pesto. In a food processor; add parsley, basil, parmesan, garlic, toasted pine nuts and salt.
2. Turn on the food processor and slowly add the olive oil.
3. Once all of the olive oil is incorporated into the pesto, store and refrigerate until ready to use.
4. Preheat the Air Fryer to 390 - degrees Fahrenheit.
5. Slice the tomato and the feta into 1/2 -inch thick circular slices. Pat tomato dry with a paper towel.
6. Spread 1 tablespoon of the pesto on top of each tomato slice and top with the feta.
7. Toss the red onions with 1 tablespoon of olive oil and place on top of the feta.
8. Place the tomatoes/feta into the cooking basket and cook for 12 – 14 minutes or until the feta starts to soften and brown.
9. Finish with a pinch of salt and an additional spoonful of basil pesto.

Cilantro Brussels Sprouts

Preparation Time: 5 minutes

Cooking time: 25 minutes

Servings: 4

Ingredients:

- 2 pounds Brussels sprouts, trimmed and halved
- 2 tablespoons maple syrup
- 1 tablespoon cilantro, chopped

- 1 tablespoon olive oil
- 1 tablespoon sweet paprika
- A pinch of salt and black pepper

Directions:

1. In your air fryer's basket, combine the sprouts with the oil, maple syrup and the remaining Ingredients:, toss and cook at 360 degrees F for 25 minutes.
2. Divide between plates and serve as a side dish.

Nutrition:

Calories 174, fat 5, fiber 3, carbs 11, protein 4

Parmesan Zucchini Rounds

Preparation Time: 25 minutes

Servings: 4

Ingredients:

- 4 zucchinis; sliced
- 1 egg; whisked
- 1 ½ cups parmesan; grated
- ¼ cup parsley; chopped.

- 1 egg white; whisked
- ½ tsp. garlic powder
- Cooking spray

Directions:

1. Take a bowl and mix the egg with egg whites, parmesan, parsley and garlic powder and whisk.
2. Dredge each zucchini slice in this mix, place them all in your air fryer's basket, grease them with cooking spray and cook at 370 °F for 20 minutes
3. Divide between plates and serve as a side dish.

Nutrition:

Calories: 183; Fat: 6g; Fiber: 2g; Carbs: 3g; Protein: 8g

Amazing Onion Rings

Preparation Time: 30 minutes

Servings: 8

Ingredients:

- 2 medium-sized eggs
- 2 medium-sized yellow onions; cut into rings
- 2 cups white flour
- 1/2 teaspoon baking soda
- 1 teaspoon baking powder
- 1 ½ teaspoons sea salt flakes
- 1 ½ cups plain milk
- 1 ¼ cups seasoned breadcrumbs
- 1/2 teaspoon dried dill weed
- 1/4 teaspoon paprika
- 1/2 teaspoon green peppercorns; freshly cracked

Directions:

1. Begin by preheating your Air Fryer to 356 - degrees Fahrenheit.

2. Place the onion rings into the bowl with icy cold water and let them stay 15 to 20 minutes.
3. Drain the onion rings and dry them using a kitchen towel.
4. In a shallow bowl; mix the sifted flour together with baking soda, baking powder and sea salt flakes.
5. Then; coat each onion ring with the flour mixture.
6. In another shallow bowl; beat the eggs with milk, add the mixture to the remaining flour mixture and whisk well. Dredge the coated onion rings into this batter.
7. In a third bowl; mix the seasoned breadcrumbs, green peppercorns, dill, and paprika. Roll the onion rings over the breadcrumb mix, covering well. Air-fry them in the cooking basket for 8 to 11 minutes or until thoroughly cooked to golden.

Tasty Turkey Wrapped Prawns

Preparation Time: 30 minutes

Servings: 2

Ingredients:

- 1 Pound. Turkey [sliced]
- 1 Pound. Prawns [tiger]

Directions:

1. Preheat Air Fryer to 390 - degrees Fahrenheit.
2. Wrap prawns with Turkey and secure with toothpick. Refrigerate for 20 minutes.
3. Cook for 10 minutes in batches. Serve with tartar sauce and enjoy the yummy taste.

Scallops with Spinach

Preparation Time: 20 minutes

Cooking Time: 10 minutes

Servings: 2

Ingredients:

- 1: 12-ounces package frozen spinach, thawed and drained
- 8 jumbo sea scallops
- Olive oil cooking spray
- 1 tablespoon fresh basil, chopped
- Salt and ground black pepper, as required
- ¾ cup heavy whipping cream
- 1 tablespoon tomato paste
- 1 teaspoon garlic, minced

Directions:

1. Preheat the Air fryer to 350 degree F and grease an Air fryer pan.
2. Season the scallops evenly with salt and black pepper.

3. Mix cream, tomato paste, garlic, basil, salt, and black pepper in a bowl.
4. Place spinach at the bottom of the Air fryer pan, followed by seasoned scallops and top with the cream mixture.
5. Transfer into the Air fryer and cook for about 10 minutes.
6. Dish out in a platter and serve hot.

Nutrition:

Calories: 203, Fat: 18.3g, Carbohydrates: 12.3g, Sugar: 1.7g, Protein: 26.4g, Sodium: 101mg

Crispy Halibut

Preparation time: 40 minutes

Servings: 4

Ingredients:

- Halibut fillets: 4
- Fresh parsley: .5 cup
- Fresh chives: .25 cup

- Pork rinds: .75 cup
- Fresh dill: .25 cup
- Black pepper & sea salt: to your liking
- Extra-virgin olive oil: 1 tbsp.
- Finely grated lemon zest: 1 tbsp.

Directions:
1. Warm the Air Fryer to reach 390º Fahrenheit.
2. Chop the chives, dill, and parsley. Combine all of the dry fixings – parsley, pork rinds, chives, dill, lemon zest, black pepper, sea salt, and olive oil.
3. Rinse the halibut well and let them drain well on paper towels.
4. Prepare a baking tin to fit in the cooker. Spoon the rinds over the fish and press in.
5. Add the prepared fillets in the fryer for 30 minutes.

Simple Lime Salmon

Preparation Time: 17 minutes

Servings: 5

Ingredients:

- 1/2 cup butter; melted
- 6 green onions; chopped.
- 2 salmon fillets; boneless
- 1 lime; sliced
- 1/2 cup olive oil
- 3 garlic cloves; minced
- 2 shallots; chopped.
- Juice of 1 lime
- Salt and black pepper to taste

Directions:

1. In a bowl, mix the salmon with the lime juice, butter, oil, garlic, shallots, salt, pepper and the green onions; rub well
2. Transfer the fish to your air fryer, top with the lime slices and cook at 380°F for 6 minutes on each side. Serve with a side salad.

Turkey and Spring Onions

Preparation Time: 40 minutes

Servings: 2

Ingredients:

- 2 small turkey breasts; boneless and skinless
- 2 red chilies; chopped.
- 1 bunch spring onions; chopped.
- 1 tbsp. Chinese rice wine
- 1 tbsp. oyster sauce
- 1 cup chicken stock
- 1 tbsp. olive oil
- 1 tbsp. soy sauce

Directions:

1. Add the oil to a pan that fits your air fryer and place it over medium heat
2. Then add the chilies, spring onions, oyster sauce, soy sauce, stock and rice wine; whisk and simmer for 3-4 minutes
3. Add the turkey, toss and place the pan in the air fryer and cook at 380 °F for 30 minutes. Divide everything between plates and serve.

Soy Sauce Chicken

Preparation Time: 50 minutes

Servings: 6

Ingredients:

- 1 whole chicken; cut into pieces
- 2 tsp. soy sauce
- 1 tsp. sesame oil
- 1 chili pepper; minced
- 1 tbsp. ginger; grated
- Salt and black pepper to taste

Directions:

1. In a bowl, mix the chicken with all the other ingredients and rub well
2. Transfer the chicken pieces to your air fryer's basket
3. Cook at 400 °F for 30 minutes and then at 380°F for 10 minutes more. Divide everything between plates and serve

Delicious Chicken Casserole

Preparation Time: 10 minutes

Cooking Time: 32 minutes

Serve: 8

Ingredients:

- 6 oz cream cheese, softened
- 2 lbs cooked chicken, shredded
- 4 oz butter, melted
- 6 oz ham, cut into small pieces
- 5 oz Swiss cheese
- 1 oz fresh lemon juice
- 1 tbsp Dijon mustard
- 1/2 tsp salt

Directions:

1. Preheat the air fryer to 325 F.
2. Arrange chicken in the bottom of air fryer baking dish then layer ham pieces on top.

3. Add butter, lemon juice, mustard, cream cheese, and salt into the blender and blend until a thick sauce.
4. Spread sauce on top of chicken and ham mixture.
5. Arrange Swiss cheese slices on top of sauce. Place baking dish in the air fryer and cook for 30-32 minutes.
6. Serve and enjoy.

Nutrition:

Calories 450, Fat 29 g, Carbohydrates 2.5 g, Sugar 0.4 g, Protein 40 g, Cholesterol 170 mg

Chicken Tenderloins

Cooking Time: 12 minutes

Servings: 4

Ingredients:

- 8 chicken tenderloins
- 1 cup breadcrumbs
- 1 egg; beaten

- 2 tbsp. olive oil
- Salt and pepper to taste

Directions:

1. Preheat your air fryer to 350 °F. Mix olive oil, breadcrumbs, pepper and salt in a bowl. Add the beaten egg in another dish
2. Dip chicken into egg then coat with breadcrumbs and place into air fryer basket and cook for 12 minutes.

Sweet and Spicy Chicken Wings

Cooking Time: 16 minutes

Servings: 6

Ingredients:

- 2 garlic cloves; chopped.
- 6 chicken wings
- 1 tbsp. honey
- 2 tbsp. Worcestershire sauce

- 1 tsp. red chili flakes
- Salt and pepper to taste

Directions:

1. Mix in a bowl, garlic, red chili flakes, honey, Worcestershire sauce, salt and pepper. Toss chicken wings in mixture and place into the fridge for an hour
2. Place the marinated chicken wings in the air fryer basket and spray them with cooking spray. Air fry chicken wings at 320 °F for 8 minutes
3. After 8 minutes, turn the heat to 350°F for another 4 minutes. Serve hot!

Chicken Kebabs

Cooking Time: 15 to 20 minutes

Servings: 5

Ingredients:
- 1 large yellow bell pepper; diced
- 2 chicken breasts; diced
- 1 large green bell pepper; diced
- 1 large red bell pepper; diced
- 3 button mushrooms; sliced
- Pepper; to taste
- 1/2 cup soy sauce
- 1/4 cup honey
- Sesame oil
- Sesame seeds
- Oil spray
- Salt; to taste

Directions:

1. Preheat the air fryer at 338 °F. Season the chicken breast with pepper and salt. Mist some oil onto it, then add the soy sauce and honey
2. Mix thoroughly. Add some sesame oil and drizzle the chicken mixture with sesame seeds.
3. Take out the wooden skewers and arrange the ingredients in the following order: yellow bell pepper, chicken breast, red bell pepper, mushroom, chicken breast, green bell pepper, chicken breast, yellow bell pepper, red bell pepper
4. Do this until all the ingredients have been used up. Glaze with the remaining honey soy sauce mixture.
5. Add the kebabs to the basket and cook for 15-20 minutes. Drizzle with remaining sesame seeds and serve.

Honey Mustard Cheesy Meatballs

Preparation Time: 15 minutes

Cooking Time: 15 minutes

Servings: 8

Ingredients:

- 1 pound ground beef
- 2 onions, chopped
- 4 tablespoons fresh basil, chopped
- 2 tablespoons cheddar cheese, grated
- 2 teaspoons garlic paste
- 2 teaspoons honey
- 2 teaspoons mustard
- Salt and black pepper, to taste

Directions:

1. Preheat the Air fryer to 385 °F and grease an Air fryer basket.
2. Mix all the ingredients in a bowl until well combined.

3. Shape the mixture into equal-sized balls gently and arrange the meatballs in the Air fryer basket.
4. Cook for about 15 minutes and dish out to serve warm.

Nutrition:

Calories: 134, Fat: 4.4g, Carbohydrates: 4.6g, Sugar: 2.7g, Protein: 18.2g, Sodium: 50mg

Lamb and Mustard Sauce

Preparation time: 10 minutes

Cooking time: 25 minutes

Servings: 4

Ingredients:
- 2pounds lamb chops
- 2tablespoons butter, melted

- 2 tablespoons mustard
- 1 cup beef stock
- 1 teaspoon coriander, ground
- 1 teaspoon sweet paprika
- Salt and black pepper to the taste

Directions:

1. In the air fryer's pan, mix the lamb chops with the mustard and the other ingredients, toss and cook at 400 degrees F for 25 minutes.
2. Divide the mix between plates and serve.

Nutrition:

Calories 284, Fat 14, Fiber 4, Carbs 17, Protein 28

Pork and Chives

Preparation Time: 32 minutes

Servings: 6

Ingredients:

- 1 lb. pork tenderloin; cubed
- 1/4 cup tarragon; chopped.
- 2 tbsp. mustard
- 2 tbsp. chives; chopped.
- 1 cup mayonnaise
- 2 garlic cloves; minced
- Salt and black pepper to taste

Directions:

1. Place all ingredients except the mayo into a pan that fits your air fryer; mix well.
2. Put the pan in the fryer and cook at 400 °F for 15 minutes
3. Add the mayo and toss
4. Put the pan in the fryer for 7 more minutes. Divide into bowls and serve.

Cumin Beef

Preparation Time: 40 minutes

Servings: 4

Ingredients:

- 4 oz. canned kidney beans; drained
- 1 lb. ground beef
- 2 garlic cloves; minced
- 2 tbsp. olive oil

- 2 tsp. cumin; ground
- 8 oz. canned tomatoes; chopped.
- 1 yellow onion; chopped.
- Salt and black pepper to taste

Directions:
1. Heat up the oil in a pan that fits your air fryer over medium heat.
2. Add the onion and the beef, stir and cook for 2-3 minutes
3. Then add the garlic, salt, pepper, beans, tomatoes and the cumin; toss and cook for another 2 minutes
4. Transfer the pan to your air fryer and cook at 380°F for 30 minutes. Divide everything into bowls and serve.

Pork Chops with Peanut Sauce

Servings: 4

Preparation Time: 20 minutes

Cooking Time: 12 minutes

Ingredients

For Chops:

- 1 teaspoon fresh ginger, minced
- 1 garlic clove, minced
- 1 tablespoon olive oil
- 2 tablespoons soy sauce
- 1 teaspoon hot pepper sauce
- 1-pound boneless pork chop, cubed into 1-inch size

For Peanut Sauce:

- 1 tablespoon olive oil
- 1 garlic clove, minced
- 1 shallot, finely chopped
- 1 teaspoon ground coriander
- ¾ cup ground peanuts
- 1 teaspoon hot pepper sauce

- ¾ cup coconut milk

Directions:
1. For pork: in a bowl, mix together the ginger, garlic, soy sauce, oil, and hot pepper sauce.
2. Add the pork chops and generously coat with mixture.
3. Place at the room temperature for about 15 minutes.
4. Set the temperature of air fryer to 390 degrees F. Grease an air fryer basket.
5. Arrange chops into the prepared air fryer basket in a single layer.
6. Air fry for about 12 minutes.
7. Meanwhile, for the sauce: in a pan, heat oil over medium heat and sauté the shallot and garlic for about 2-3 minutes.
8. Add the coriander and sauté for about 1 minute.
9. Stir in the remaining ingredients and cook for about 5 minutes, stirring continuously.
10. Remove the pan of sauce from heat and let it

cool slightly.

11. Remove the chops from air fryer and transfer onto serving plates.
12. Serve immediately with the topping of peanut sauce.

Nutrition:

Calories: 725, Carbohydrate: 9.5g, Protein: 34.4g, Fat: 62.9g, Sugar: 2.8g, Sodium: 543mg

Pork Shoulder with Pineapple Sauce

Servings: 3

Preparation Time: 20 minutes

Cooking Time: 24 minutes

Ingredients

For Pork:

- 10½ ounces pork shoulder, cut into bite-sized pieces
- 1 egg
- 2 pinches of Maggi seasoning
- 1 teaspoon light soy sauce
- Dash of sesame oil
- ¼ cup plain flour

For Sauce:

- 1 medium onion, sliced
- 1 medium tomato, chopped
- 1 teaspoon olive oil
- 1 tablespoon garlic, minced
- 1 large pineapple slice, cubed
- 2 tablespoons tomato sauce

- 2 tablespoons oyster sauce
- 1 tablespoon Worcestershire sauce
- 1 teaspoon sugar
- 1 tablespoon water
- ½ tablespoon corn flour

Directions:
1. For pork: in a large bowl, mix together the Maggi seasoning, soy sauce, and sesame oil.
2. Add the pork cubes and generously mix with the mixture.
3. Refrigerate to marinate for about 4-6 hours.
4. In a shallow dish, beat the egg.
5. In another dish, place the plain flour.
6. Dip the cubed pork in beaten egg and then, coat evenly with the flour.
7. Set the temperature of air fryer to 248 degrees F. Grease an air fryer basket.
8. Arrange pork cubes into the prepared air fryer basket in a single layer.
9. Air fry for about 20 minutes.

10. Meanwhile, for the sauce: in a skillet, heat oil over medium heat and sauté the onion and garlic for about 1 minute.
11. Add the pineapple, and tomato and cook for about 1 minute.
12. Add the tomato sauce, oyster sauce, Worcestershire sauce, and sugar and stir to combine.
13. Meanwhile, in a bowl, mix together the water and corn flour.
14. Add the corn flour mixture into the sauce, stirring continuously.
15. Cook until the sauce is thicken enough, stirring continuously.
16. Remove pork cubes from air fryer and add into the sauce.
17. Cook for about 1-2 minutes or until coated completely.
18. Remove from the heat and serve hot.

Nutrition:

Calories: 557, Carbohydrate: 57.5g, Protein: 28.8g, Fat: 25.1g, Sugar: 35.1g, Sodium: 544mg

(Note: If you don't have fresh pineapple in hands, then you can use canned pineapple. But remember to skip sugar from the sauce).

Milanese Veal Legs

Preparation time: 10-20 minutes,

Cooking time: more than 60 minutes;

Serve: 4

Ingredients

- 1kg beef leg
- 1 glass of white wine
- 1 onion
- 150g hot broth
- Taste Flour
- 1 bunch of parsley
- ½ grated lemon
- 1 clove garlic
- Salt, pepper to taste

Directions:

1. Place the chopped onion in the basket. Brown for 4 minutes at 150 °C.
2. Add the lightly floured ears the white wine, season with salt and pepper and simmer for 6 minutes.
3. Turn the spikes, add the broth, and cook for another 50 minutes turning the meat 1-2 times.

4. At this point, add the chopped parsley, a grated peel of half a lemon and a clove of garlic and continue cooking for the remaining 10 minutes.
5. Serve hot with the juice that has formed in the cooking vessel.

Nutrition:

Calories 499, Fat 22.54g, Carbohydrate 38.25g, Sugars 2.27g, Protein 34.23g, Cholesterol 160mg

Broccoli with Cauliflower

Preparation Time: 15 minutes

Cooking Time: 20 minutes

Servings: 4

Ingredients:

- 1½ cups broccoli, cut into 1-inch pieces
- 1½ cups cauliflower, cut into 1-inch pieces
- 1 tablespoon olive oil

- Salt, as required

Directions:

1. Preheat the Air fryer to 375 degrees F and grease an Air fryer basket.
2. Mix the vegetables, olive oil, and salt in a bowl and toss to coat well.
3. Arrange the veggie mixture in the Air fryer basket and cook for about 20 minutes, tossing once in between.
4. Dish out in a bowl and serve hot.

Nutrition:

Calories: 51, Fat: 3.7g, Carbohydrates: 4.3g, Sugar: 1.5g, Protein: 1.7g, Sodium: 61mg

Lentil Soup

Preparation Time: 6 minutes

Cooking Time: 10 minutes

Servings: 4

Ingredients:

- Spinach
- 1 Big diced onion
- 2 Tbsp of red curry paste
- 3 minced garlic cloves
- 1/8 Teaspoon of ginger powder
- 1 Tbsp of red pepper flakes
- 1 and ½ oz Can coconut milk
- 1 oz Can of cut tomatoes
- 2 Cups of broth (Vegetable broth)
- 1 and ½ Cups of Red lentils

Directions:

1. In your Air fryer cooker, click the button of the option "Sauté" and wait a couple of minutes until it becomes warm.

2. Now, add your diced onion and the garlic; then sauté altogether until the components become brown. Add a little quantity of broth.
3. Once you notice the ingredients starting to have a brown colour, press the cancelling button to stop the process of sautéing.
4. Add the paste of the red curry, the ginger powder and the red pepper flakes and keep stirring.
5. Add your coconut milk, the diced tomatoes, the vegetable broth and the lentils and stir again.
6. Now, lock the lid and the button "Manual" then reduce your timer to around 7 minutes.
7. Let the pressure in the pot release naturally.
8. Once the steam is released, open the Air fryer and add the spinach
9. Serve and enjoy your soup.

Nutrition:

Calories – 120 Protein – 8 g. Fat – 1.5 g. Carbs – 20 g.

Mediterranean Bamyeh Okra Tomato Stew

Preparation Time: 5 minutes

Cooking Time: 7 minutes

Servings: 4

Ingredients:

- ¼ cup of water
- 2 tablespoons apple cider vinegar
- 1 cup onions, chopped
- 1 tablespoon minced garlic
- ounce canned tomatoes
- 1 tablespoon vegetable broth
- 1 teaspoon smoked paprika
- ½ teaspoon ground allspice
- 1 teaspoon salt
- 1 1/2 pounds fresh okra

Directions:

1. Place all ingredients except for the lemon juice and tomato paste into air fryer. Put in okra last.
2. Cook on high pressure for 2 minutes, let it rest for 5 minutes.
3. Quick release the pressure.
4. Open the lid carefully and add tomato paste in water and then the lemon juice. Stir gently and serve.

Nutrition:

Calories – 85 Protein – 4 g. Fat – 5 g. Carbs – 19 g.

Herbed Eggplant (Vegan)

Servings: 2

Preparation Time: 15 minutes

Cooking Time: 15 minutes

Ingredients

- ½ teaspoon dried marjoram, crushed
- ½ teaspoon dried oregano, crushed
- ½ teaspoon garlic powder
- ½ teaspoon dried thyme, crushed
- 1 large eggplant, cubed
- Olive oil cooking spray
- Salt and ground black pepper, as required

Directions:

1. Set the temperature of air fryer to 390 degrees F. Grease an air fryer basket.
2. In a small bowl, mix well herbs, garlic powder, salt, and black pepper.
3. Spray the eggplant cubes evenly with cooking spray and then, rub with the herbs mixture.

4. Arrange eggplant cubes into the prepared air fryer basket in a single layer.
5. Air fry for about 6 minutes.
6. Flip and spray the eggplant cubes with cooking spray.
7. Air fry for another 6 minutes.
8. Flip and again, spray the eggplant cubes with cooking spray.
9. Air fry for 2-3 more minutes.
10. Remove from air fryer and transfer the eggplant cubes onto serving plates.
11. Serve hot.

Nutrition:

Calories: 62, Carbohydrate: 14.5g, Protein: 2.4g, Fat: 0.5g, Sugar: 7.1g, Sodium: 83mg

Grilled Buffalo Cauliflower (Vegan)

Servings: 1

Cooking Time: 5 minutes

Ingredients:

- 1 cup cauliflower florets
- ½ cup buffalo sauce
- Cooking oil spray

- Salt and pepper, to taste

Directions

1. Place the cauliflower florets in a bowl and spray with cooking oil. Season with salt and pepper.
2. Toss to coat.
3. Place the grill pan in the air fryer and add the cauliflower florets.
4. Close the lid and cook for 5 minutes at 390 degrees F.
5. Once cooked, place in a bowl and pour the buffalo sauce over the top. Toss to coat.

Nutrition

Calories: 25; Carbs: 5.3g; Protein: 2g; Fat: 0.1g

Greatest Green Beans (Vegan)

Servings: 1

Cooking Time: 5 minutes

Ingredients:

- 1 cup green beans, trimmed
- ½ teaspoon oil
- Salt and pepper, to taste

Directions

1. Place the green beans in a bowl and add in oil, salt, and pepper.
2. Toss to coat the beans.
3. Place the grill pan in the air fryer and add the green beans in a single layer.
4. Close the lid and cook for 5 minutes at 390 degrees F.

Nutrition

Calories: 54; Carbs: 7.7g; Protein: 2g; Fat: 2.5g

Summer Grilled Corn (Vegan)

Servings: 2

Cooking Time: 6 minutes

Ingredients:

- 2 corn on the cob, cut into halves widthwise
- ½ teaspoon oil
- Salt and pepper, to taste

Directions

1. Brush the corn cobs with oil and season with salt and pepper.
2. Place the grill pan accessory into the air fryer.
3. Place the corn cobs on the grill pan.
4. Close the lid and cook for 3 minutes at 390 degrees F.
5. Open the air fryer and turn the corn cobs.
6. Cook for another 3 minutes at the same temperature.

Nutrition

Calories: 173; Carbs: 29g; Protein: 4.5 g; Fat: 4.5g

Bacon Wrapped Brie

Preparation Time: 15 minutes

Servings: 8

Ingredients:

- 1: 8-oz.round Brie
- 4 slices sugar-free bacon.

Directions:

1. Place two slices of bacon to form an X. Place the third slice of bacon horizontally across the center of the X. Place the fourth slice of bacon vertically across the X. It should look like a plus sign: +on top of an X. Place the Brie in the center of the bacon
2. Wrap the bacon around the Brie, securing with a few toothpicks. Cut a piece of parchment to fit your air fryer basket and place the bacon-wrapped Brie on top. Place inside the air fryer basket.

3. Adjust the temperature to 400 Degrees F and set the timer for 10 minutes. When 3 minutes remain on the timer, carefully flip Brie
4. When cooked, bacon will be crispy and cheese will be soft and melty. To serve; cut into eight slices.

Nutrition:

Calories: 116; Protein: 7.7g; Fiber: 0.0g; Fat: 8.9g; Carbs: 0.2g

Garlic Cheese Dip

Preparation Time: 15 minutes

Servings: 10

Ingredients:

- 1 lb. mozzarella; shredded
- 6 garlic cloves; minced
- 3 tbsp. olive oil
- 1 tsp. rosemary; chopped.
- 1 tbsp. thyme; chopped.
- A pinch of salt and black pepper

Directions:

1. In a pan that fits your air fryer, mix all the ingredients, whisk really well, introduce in the air fryer and cook at 370 °F for 10 minutes.
2. Divide into bowls and serve right away.

Nutrition:

Calories: 184; Fat: 11g; Fiber: 3g; Carbs: 5g; Protein: 7g

Heirloom Tomato Sandwiches with Pesto

Preparation Time: 20 minutes

Cooking Time: 16 minutes

Servings: 4

Ingredients:

- 3 tablespoons pine nuts
- 2 heirloom tomatoes, cut into ½ inch thick slices
- 1 garlic clove, chopped
- 8-ounce feta cheese, cut into ½ inch thick slices
- ½ cup fresh basil, chopped
- ½ cup fresh parsley, chopped
- ½ cup plus 2 tablespoons olive oil, divided
- Salt, to taste

Directions:

1. Preheat the Air fryer to 390 degrees F and grease an Air fryer basket.
2. Mix together 1 tablespoon of olive oil, pine nuts and pinch of salt in a bowl.

3. Place pine nuts in the Air fryer and cook for about 2 minutes.
4. Put the pine nuts, remaining oil, fresh basil, fresh parsley, garlic and salt and pulse until combined.
5. Dish out the pesto in a bowl, cover and refrigerate.
6. Spread 1 tablespoon of pesto on each tomato slice and top with a feta slice and onion.
7. Drizzle with olive oil and arrange the prepared tomato slices in the Air fryer basket.
8. Cook for about 14 minutes and serve with remaining pesto.

Nutrition:

Calories: 559, Fat: 55.7g, Carbohydrates: 8g, Sugar: 2.6g, Protein: 11.8g, Sodium: 787mg

Tofu in Sweet and Spicy Sauce

Preparation Time: 15 minutes

Cooking Time: 6 minutes

Servings: 2

Ingredients:

- 1: 14-ouncesblock firm tofu, pressed and cubed
- 2 scallions: green part), chopped
- ½ cup arrowroot flour
- ½ teaspoon sesame oil
- 4 tablespoons low-sodium soy sauce
- 1½ tablespoons rice vinegar
- 1½ tablespoons chili sauce
- 1 tablespoon agave nectar
- 2 large garlic cloves, minced
- 1 teaspoon fresh ginger, peeled and grated

Directions:

1. Preheat the Air fryer to 360 degrees F and grease an Air fryer basket.

2. Mix together tofu, arrowroot flour, and sesame oil in a bowl.
3. Arrange the tofu into the Air fryer basket and cook for about 20 minutes.
4. Meanwhile, mix together the remaining ingredients except for scallions in a bowl to make a sauce.
5. Place the tofu and sauce in a skillet and cook for about 3 minutes, stirring occasionally.
6. Garnish with green parts of scallions and serve hot.

Nutrition:

Calories: 153, Fat: 6.4g, Carbohydrates: 13.5g, Sugar: 13.4g, Protein: 13.4g, Sodium: 1300mg

Cream and Coconut Cups

Preparation Time: 15 minutes

Servings: 6

Ingredients:

- 3 eggs
- 8 oz. cream cheese, soft
- 2 tbsp. butter; melted
- 3 tbsp. coconut, shredded and unsweetened
- 4 tbsp. swerve

Directions:

1. Take a bowl and mix all the ingredients and whisk really well.
2. Divide into small ramekins, put them in the fryer and cook at 320 °F and bake for 10 minutes. Serve cold

Nutrition:

Calories: 164; Fat: 4g; Fiber: 2g; Carbs: 5g; Protein: 5g

Apple and Cinnamon Sauce

Preparation Time: 40 minutes

Servings: 6

Ingredients:

- 6 apples; peeled, cored and cut into wedges
- 1 cup red wine
- 1 cup sugar
- 1 tbsp. cinnamon powder

Directions:

1. In a pan that fits your air fryer, place all of the ingredients and toss
2. Place the pan in the fryer and cook at 320°F for 30 minutes. Divide into cups and serve right away

Oriental Coconut Cake

Servings: 8

Cooking Time: 40 minutes

Ingredients

- 2 eggs
- 1 cup gluten-free flour
- 1/2 cup flaked coconut
- 1-1/2 teaspoons baking powder
- 1/2 teaspoon baking soda
- 1/2 teaspoon xanthan gum
- 1/2 teaspoon salt
- 1/2 cup coconut milk
- 1/2 cup vegetable oil
- 1/2 teaspoon vanilla extract
- 1/4 cup chopped walnuts
- 3/4 cup white sugar

Directions:

1. In blender blend all wet Ingredients. Add dry ingredients and blend thoroughly.
2. Lightly grease baking pan of air fryer with cooking spray.
3. Pour in batter. Cover pan with foil.
4. For 30 minutes, cook on 330 °F.
5. Let it rest for 10 minutes
6. Serve and enjoy.

Nutrition:

Calories: 359; Carbs: 35.2g; Protein: 4.3g; Fat: 22.3g

Pound Cake with Fresh Apples

Servings: 6

Cooking Time: 60 minutes

Ingredients

- 1 medium Granny Smith apples - peeled, cored and chopped
- 1 cup white sugar
- 1 teaspoon vanilla extract
- 1-1/2 eggs
- 1-1/2 cups all-purpose flour
- 1/2 teaspoon baking soda
- 1/4 teaspoon ground cinnamon
- 2/3 cup and 1 tablespoon chopped walnuts
- 1/2 teaspoon salt
- 3/4 cup vegetable oil

Directions:

1. In blender, blend all ingredients except for apples and walnuts. Blend thoroughly. Fold in apples and walnuts.

2. Lightly grease baking pan of air fryer with cooking spray. Pour batter.
3. Cover pan with foil.
4. For 30 minutes, cook on preheated 330 °F air fryer.
5. Remove foil and cook for another 20 minutes.
6. Let it stand for 10 minutes.
7. Serve and enjoy.

Nutrition:

Calories: 696; Carbs: 71.1g; Protein: 6.5g; Fat: 42.8g

Crispy Good Peaches

Servings: 4

Cooking Time: 30 minutes

Ingredients

- teaspoon cinnamon
- teaspoon sugar, white
- 1/4 cup Flour, white
- 1/cup oats, dry rolled
- tablespoon Flour, white
- tablespoon butter, unsalted
- tablespoon sugar
- tablespoon pecans, chopped
- cup sliced peaches, frozen

Directions:

1. Lightly grease baking pan of air fryer with cooking spray. Mix in a tsp cinnamon, 2 tbsp flour, 3 tbsp sugar, and peaches.

2. For 20 minutes, cook on 300 °F.
3. Mix the rest of the Ingredients in a bowl. Pour over peaches.
4. Cook for 10 minutes at 330 °F.
5. Serve and enjoy.

Nutrition:

Calories: 435; Carbs: 74.1g; Protein: 4.3g; Fat: 13.4g

Pecan Pie

Servings: 5

Preparation Time: 15 minutes

Cooking Time: 35 minutes

Ingredients

- ¾ cup brown sugar
- ¼ cup caster sugar

- 1/3 cup butter, melted
- 2 large eggs
- 1¾ tablespoons flour
- 1 tablespoon milk
- 1 teaspoon vanilla extract
- 1 cup pecan halves
- 1 frozen pie crust, thawed

Directions:
1. In a large bowl, mix well sugars, and butter.
2. Add the eggs and whisk until foamy.
3. Add the flour, milk, and vanilla extract and whisk until well combined.
4. Fold in the pecan halves.
5. Set the temperature of air fryer to 300 degrees F. Grease a pie pan.
6. Arrange the crust in the bottom of prepared pie pan.
7. Transfer pecan mixture evenly over the crust.
8. Arrange the pan in an air fryer basket.

9. Air fry for about 22 minutes and then, another 13 minutes at 285 degrees F.
10. Remove from air fryer and place the pie pan onto a wire rack to cool for about 10-15 minutes before serving.
11. Serve warm.

Nutrition:

Calories: 575, Carbohydrate: 49.9g, Protein: 6.9g, Fat: 40.5g, Sugar: 33.5g, Sodium: 286mg

Blueberry Muffins

Servings: 5

Preparation Time: 10 minutes

Cooking Time: 14 minutes

Ingredients:

- 1 egg
- 3/4 cup blueberries
- 1/3 cup almond milk

- 3 tbsp grass-fed butter, melted
- 1 tsp vanilla
- 2 tbsp erythritol
- 1 tsp baking powder
- 2/3 cup almond flour

Directions

1. Add all ingredients into the mixing bowl and mix until well combined.
2. Pour batter into the silicon muffin molds.
3. Place in air fryer and cook for 14 minutes at 320 F/ 160 C.
4. Serve and enjoy.

Nutrition Values:

Calories 212; Fat 19.1 g; Carbohydrates 12.7 g; Sugar 3.4 g; Protein 4.9 g; Cholesterol 51 mg

Vanilla Pound Cake.

Preparation Time: 35 minutes

Servings: 6

Ingredients:

- 2 large eggs.
- ½ cup full-fat sour cream.
- 1 oz. full-fat cream cheese; softened.
- ½ cup granular erythritol.
- 1 cup blanched finely ground almond flour.
- ¼ cup salted butter; melted.
- 1 tsp. baking powder.
- 1 tsp. vanilla extract.

Directions:

1. Take a large bowl, mix almond flour, butter and erythritol.
2. Add in vanilla, baking powder, sour cream and cream cheese and mix until well combined. Add eggs and mix.

3. Pour batter into a 6-inch round baking pan. Place pan into the air fryer basket. Adjust the temperature to 300 Degrees F and set the timer for 25 minutes.
4. When the cake is done, a toothpick inserted in center will come out clean. The center should not feel wet. Allow it to cool completely, or the cake will crumble when moved.

Nutrition:

Calories: 253; Protein: 6.9g; Fiber: 2.0g; Fat: 22.6g; Carbs: 25.2g

Notes

www.ingramcontent.com/pod-product-compliance
Lightning Source LLC
Chambersburg PA
CBHW070931080526
44589CB00013B/1477